CLASSICAL & MODERN WORKS

ORCHESTRAL EXCERPTS
from the Symphonic Repertoire

VOLUME I
(REVISED)

FOR CELLO

Compiled and edited by LEONARD ROSE
Additional editing by NATHAN STUTCH

Published in 2019 by Allegro Editions

Orchestral Excerpts for the Symphonic Repertoire for Cello /vol.1
ISBN: 978-1-9748-9943-2 (paperback)

Cover design by Kaitlyn Whitaker

Cover image: "*Cello*" by Mindscape Studio courtesy of Shutterstock;
"*Music Sheet*" by danielo courtesy of Shutterstock

**ALLEGRO
EDITIONS**

Contents

VOLUME I

ARENSKY	Variations on a theme by Tchaikovsky	3
BEETHOVEN	Symphony No.1	4
BEETHOVEN	Overture "Egmont"	5
BEETHOVEN	Overture "Leonore No.1"	5
BEETHOVEN	Symphony No.4	6
BEETHOVEN	Ballet Music from "Prometheus"	7
BEETHOVEN	Symphony No.9	8
BERLIOZ	Romeo and Juliet	10
BERLIOZ	Ov. "Beatrice & Benedict"	12
BERLIOZ	Hungarian March from "The Damnation of Faust"	12
BIZET	L'Arlesienne – Suite No.1	13
BRAHMS	Symphony No.1	13
BRAHMS	Symphony No.4	17
BRAHMS	Tragic Overture	20
BRUCKNER	Symphony No.4	21
CHABRIER	España	23
CHAUSSON	Symphony in B flat	23
DEBUSSY	Nocturnes	25
DUKAS	The Sorcerer's Apprentice	27
DVOŘÁK	Symphony No.5 "New World"	29
ELGAR	Enigma Variations	30
DE FALLA	The Three-Cornered Hat	32
FAURÉ	Pelleas et Melisande	33
HAYDN	Symphony No.94 ("Surprise")	33
HAYDN	Symphony No.45 ("Farewell")	34
HUMPERDINCK	Prelude to "Hansel & Gretel"	34
KABALEVSKY	Overture 'Colas Breugnon'	35
LALO	Overture 'Le Roi d'Ys'	36
LISZT	Piano Concerto No.1	36
MAHLER	Symphony No.1	37
MENDELSSOHN	Symphony No.5 "Reformation"	38
MENDELSSOHN	Scherzo from "Midsummer Night's Dream"	39
MENDELSSOHN	Wedding March from "Midsummer Night's Dream"	39
MENDELSSOHN	Finale from "Midsummer Night's Dream"	40
MENDELSSOHN	Overture "Fingal's Cave"	40
MOZART	Symphony No.40	40
MOZART	Overture "Magic Flute"	41
NICOLAI	Overture "Merry Wives of Windsor"	41
PROKOFIEFF	Classical Symphony	42
RIMSKY-KORSAKOV	Overture "Russian Easter"	43
ROSSINI	Ov. "William Tell"	43
RIMSKY-KORSAKOV	Suite "Le Coq d'Or"	44
SAINT-SAËNS	Bacchanale from "Samson and Dalilah"	44
SCHUBERT	Unfinished Symphony	45
SCHUMANN	Symphony No.1	46
SCHUMANN	Overture "Manfred"	46
SHOSTAKOVICH	Symphony No.1	47
SIBELIUS	Symphony No.1	48
SIBELIUS	The Swan of Tuonela	50
SMETANA	Moldau	50
STRAUSS	Emperor Waltz	51
STRAVINSKY	Petrouchka	52
SUPPÉ	Overture "Poet and Peasant"	53
TCHAIKOVSKY	The Swan Lake	54
TCHAIKOVSKY	Symphony No.4	54
TCHAIKOVSKY	Nutcracker Suite	58
WAGNER	Faust Overture	59
WEBER	Overture "Oberon"	61

Variations on a theme by Tchaikovsky

ANTON ARENSKY, Op. 35a

SYMPHONY No. 1

L. VAN BEETHOVEN, Op. 21

Overture "Egmont"

L. VAN BEETHOVEN, Op. 84

Overture "Leonore No. 1"

L. VAN BEETHOVEN, Op. 138

SYMPHONY No. 4

L. VAN BEETHOVEN, Op. 60

Ballet Music from "PROMETHEUS"

L. VAN BEETHOVEN, Op. 43

SYMPHONY No. 9

L. VAN BEETHOVEN, Op. 125

9

Romeo and Juliet

Allegro fugato ♩ = 116

HECTOR BERLIOZ, Op. 9

Overture "Beatrice and Benedict"

Allegro scherzando (M.M. ♩. = 66) **HECTOR BERLIOZ**

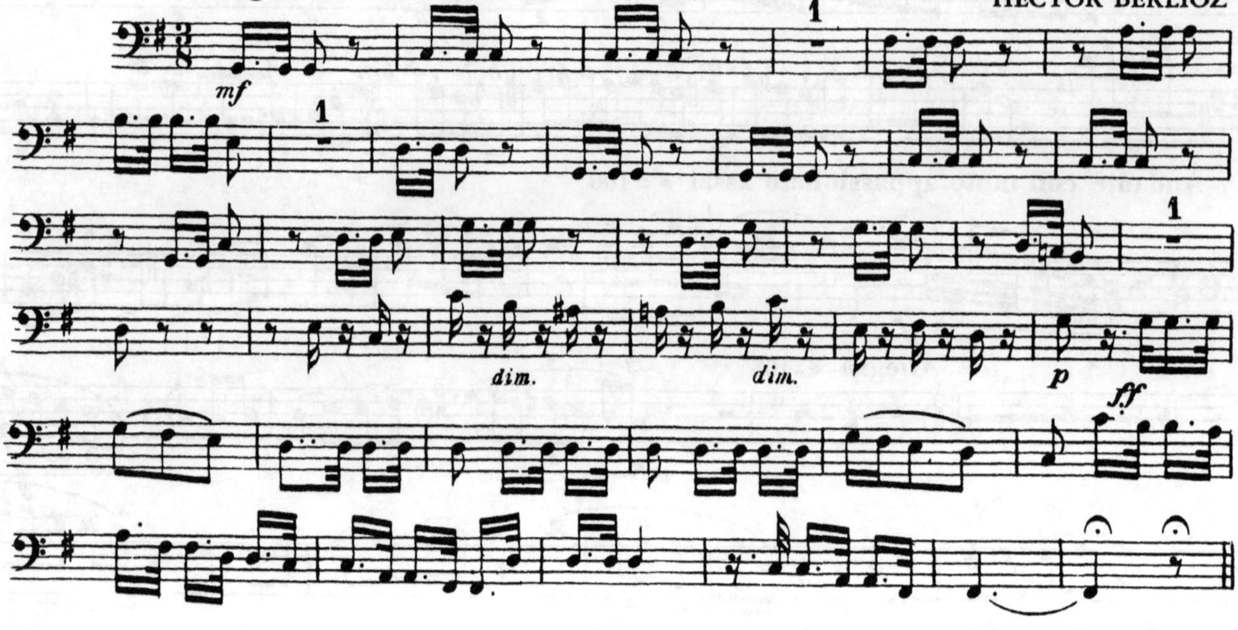

Hungarian March from "The Damnation of Faust"

Allegro marcato (𝅗𝅥 = 88) **HECTOR BERLIOZ, Op. 24**

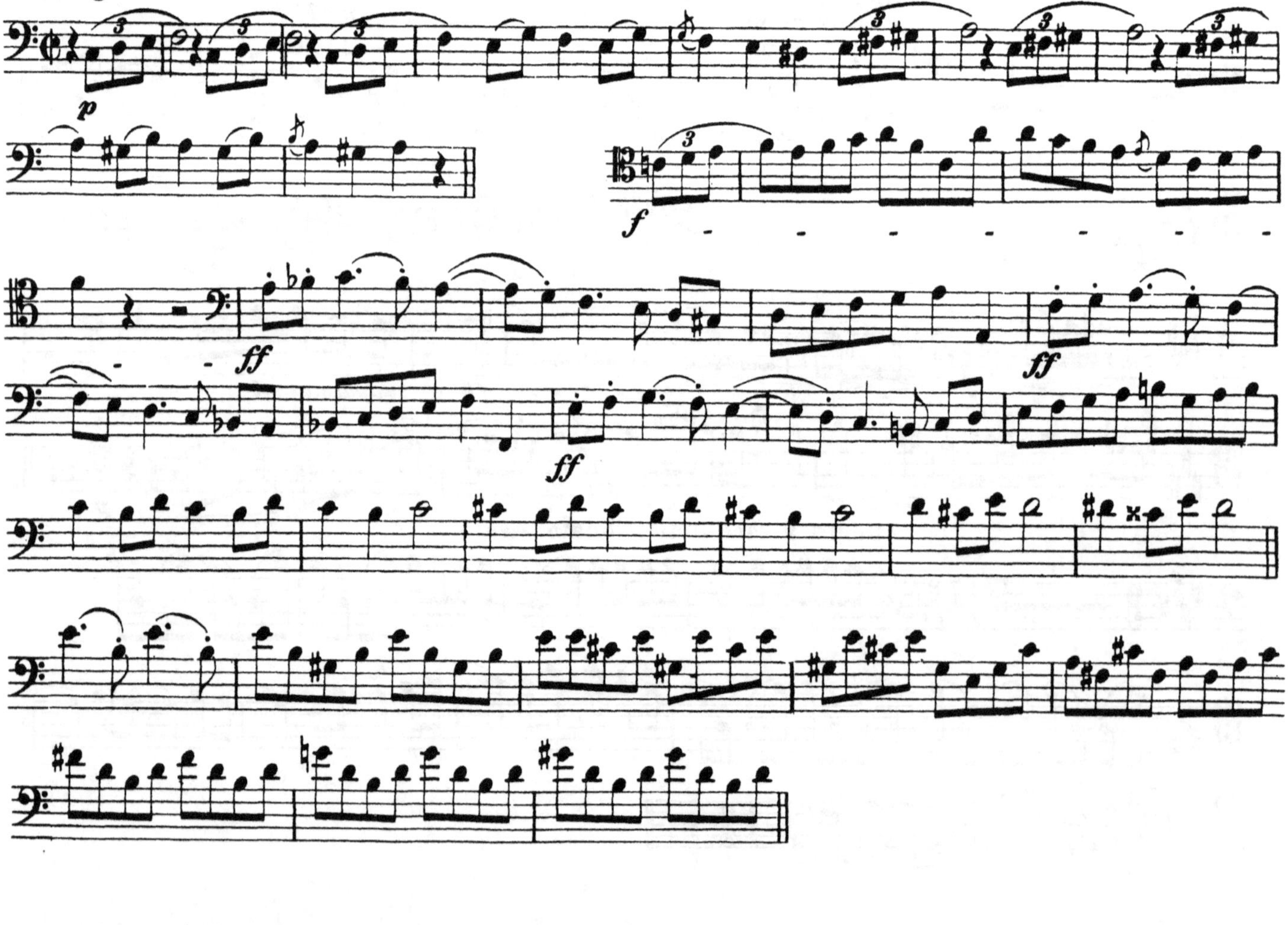

SYMPHONY No. 4

Allegro non troppo   JOHANNES BRAHMS, Op. 98

TRAGIC OVERTURE

JOHANNES BRAHMS, Op. 81

SYMPHONY No. 4

ANTON BRUCKNER

ESPAÑA

Allegro con fuoco — EMMANUEL CHABRIER

SYMPHONY

ERNEST CHAUSSON, Op. 20

3. Sirènes

THE SORCERER'S APPRENTICE

PAUL DUKAS

SYMPHONY No. 5
("New World")

ANTONIN DVOŘÁK, Op. 95

ENIGMA VARIATIONS

EDWARD ELGAR, Op. 36

Suite from "The Three-Cornered Hat"

MANUEL DE FALLA

"Pelleas and Melisande"

SYMPHONY No. 94 ("Surprise")

SYMPHONY No. 45

("Farewell")

FRANZ JOSEF HAYDN

Prelude to

"HANSEL AND GRETEL"

Allegro

ENGELBERT HUMPERDINCK

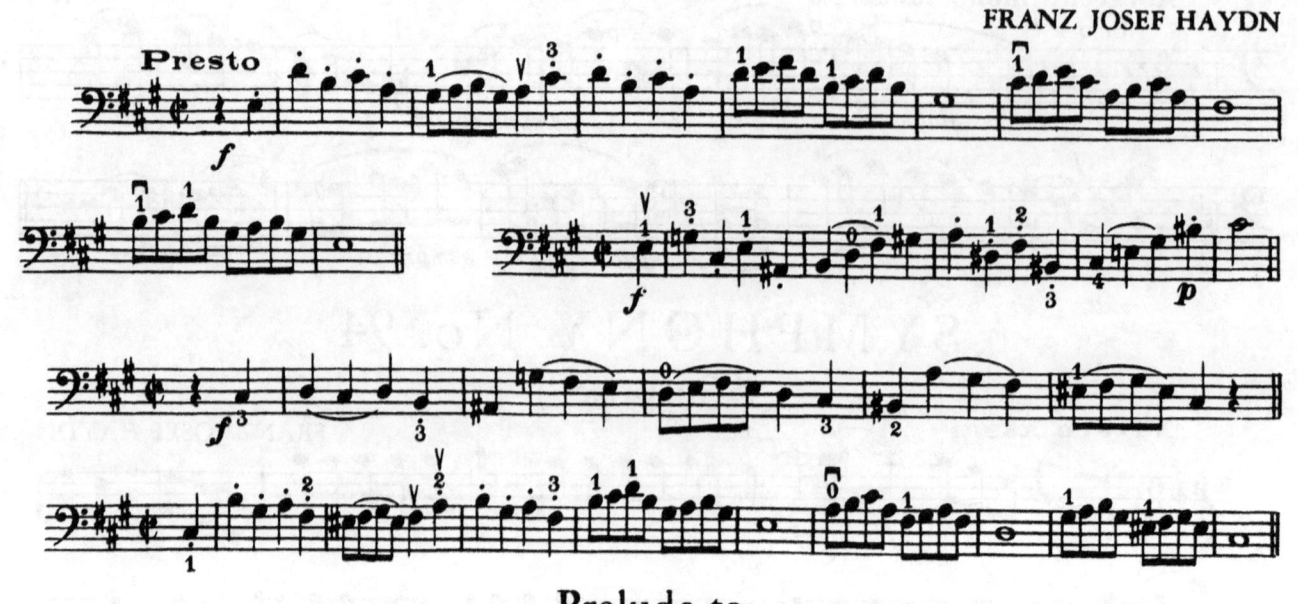

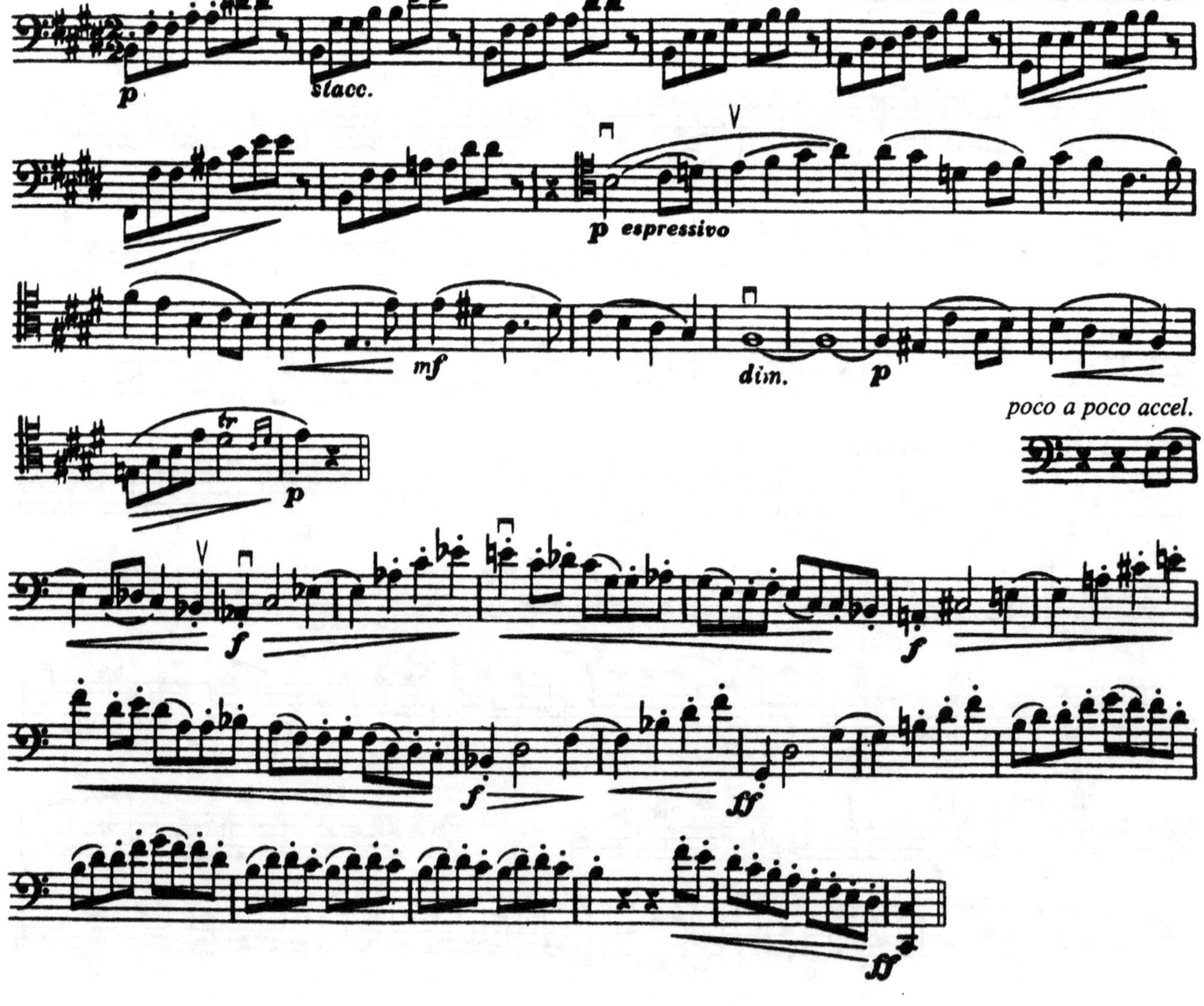

Overture
"Colas Breugnon"

DMITRI KABALEVSKY

Overture "Le Roi d'Ys"

EDOUARD LALO

Piano Concerto No. 1

FRANZ LISZT

SYMPHONY No. 1

GUSTAV MAHLER

SYMPHONY No. 5
("Reformation")

FELIX MENDELSSOHN, Op. 107

Scherzo
from "Midsummer Night's Dream"

FELIX MENDELSSOHN, Op. 61

Wedding March
from "Midsummer Night's Dream"

FELIX MENDELSSOHN, Op. 61

Finale
from "Midsummer Night's Dream"

FELIX MENDELSSOHN, Op. 61

Overture "FINGAL'S CAVE"
("Hebrides")

Allegro moderato

FELIX MENDELSSOHN, Op. 26

SYMPHONY No. 40

Allegro molto

W. A. MOZART K. 550

Overture "Magic Flute"

W. A. MOZART, K.620

Overture "Merry Wives of Windsor"

KARL NICOLAI

CLASSICAL SYMPHONY

SERGEI PROKOFIEFF, Op. 25

Overture "RUSSIAN EASTER"

Lento mystico

NIKOLAI RIMSKY-KORSAKOV, Op. 36

Overture "William Tell"

Andante

GIOACCHINO ROSSINI

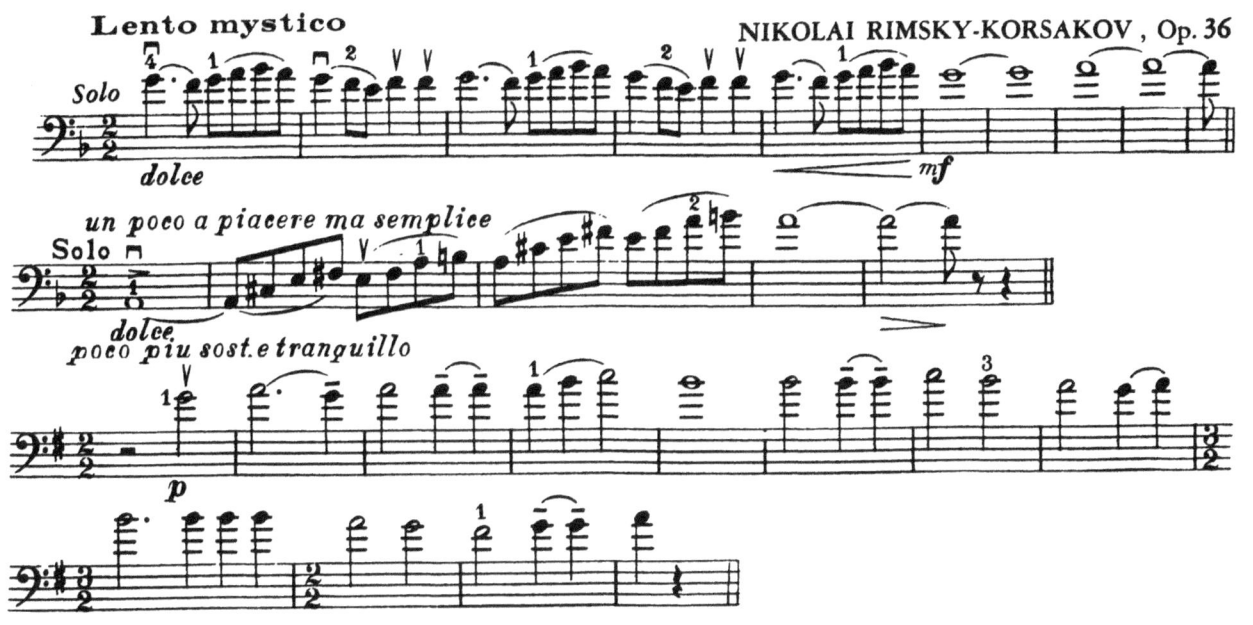

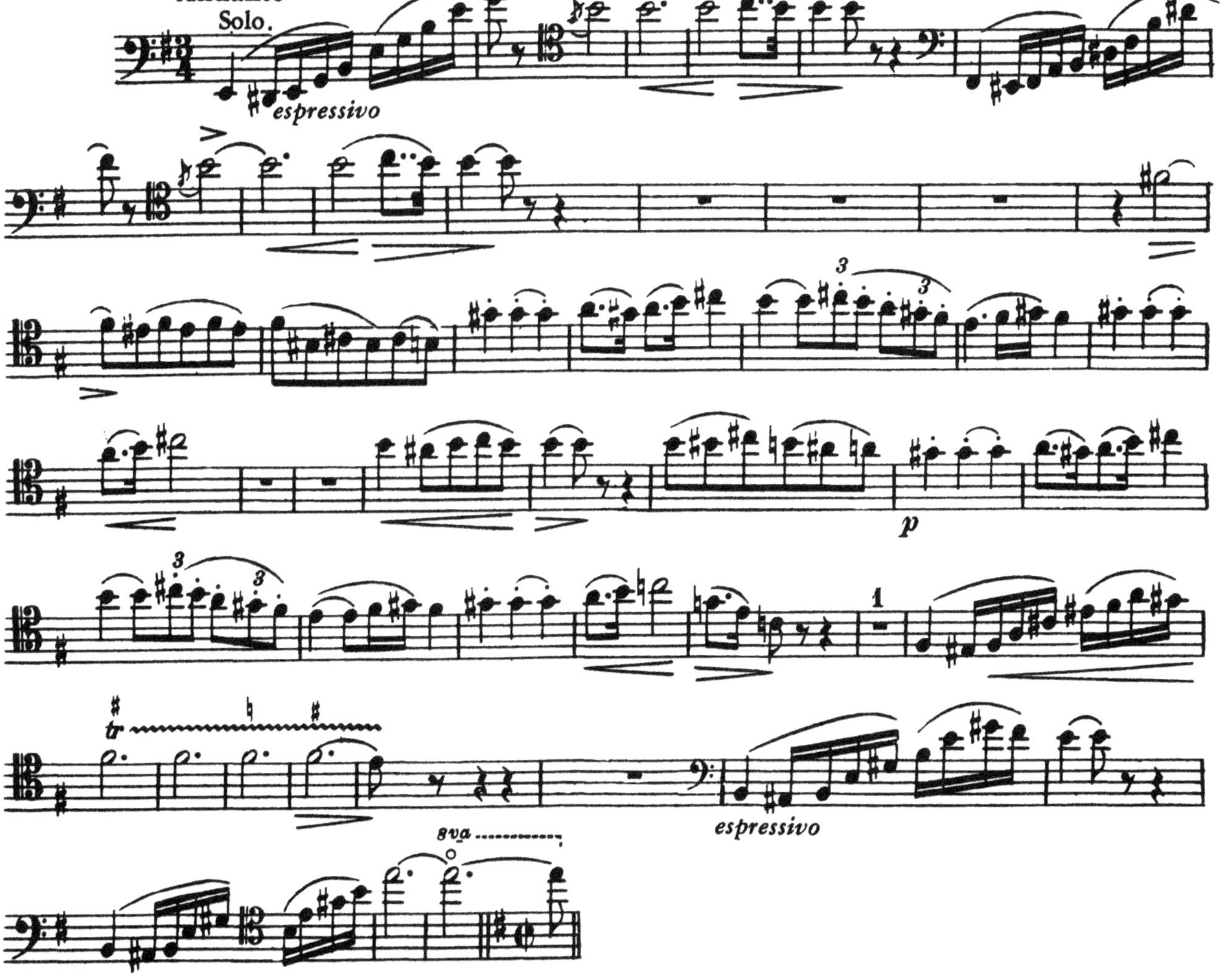

Suite from "LE COQ D'OR"

Lento

NIKOLAI RIMSKY-KORSAKOV

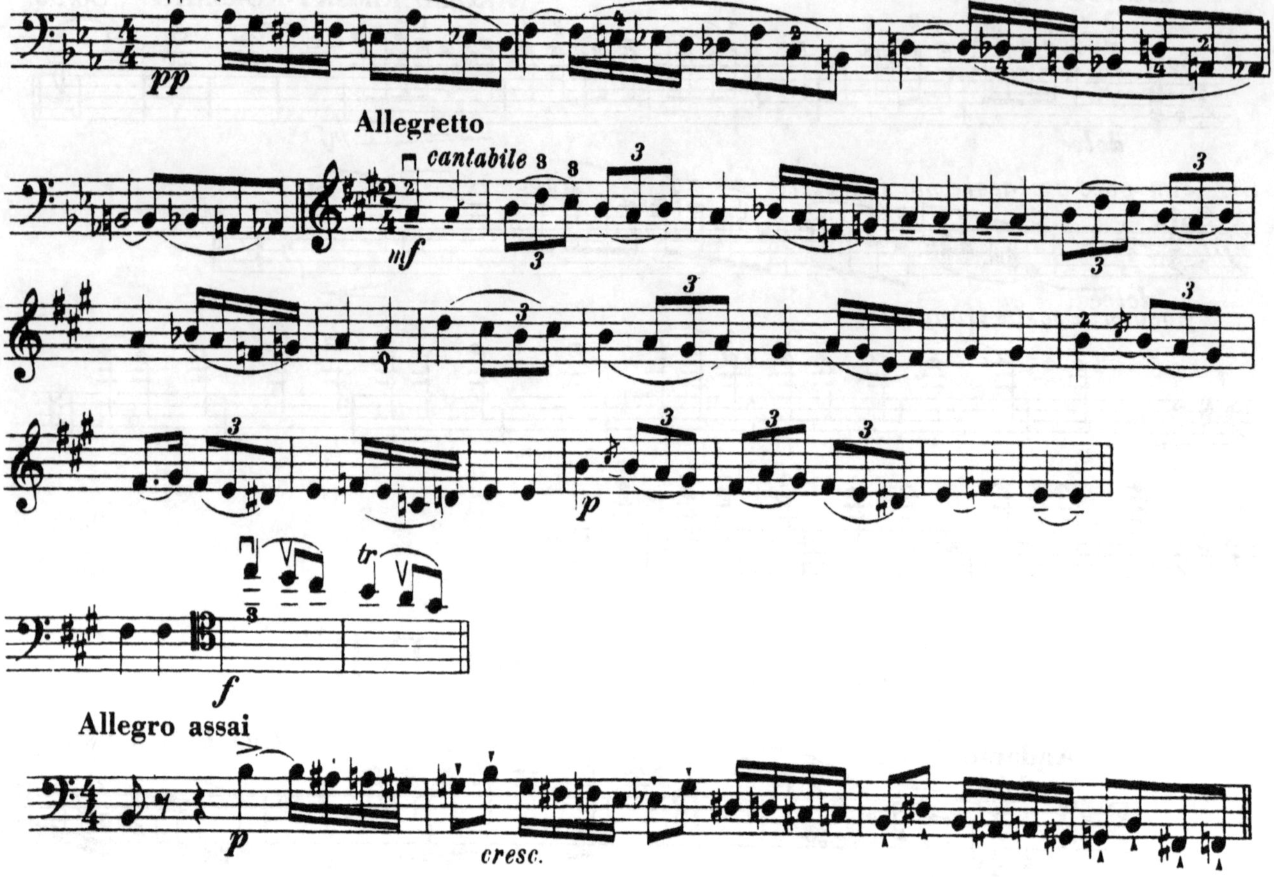

Bacchanale from "Samson and Delilah"

Allegro moderato (♩ = 120)

CAMILLE SAINT-SAENS, Op. 47

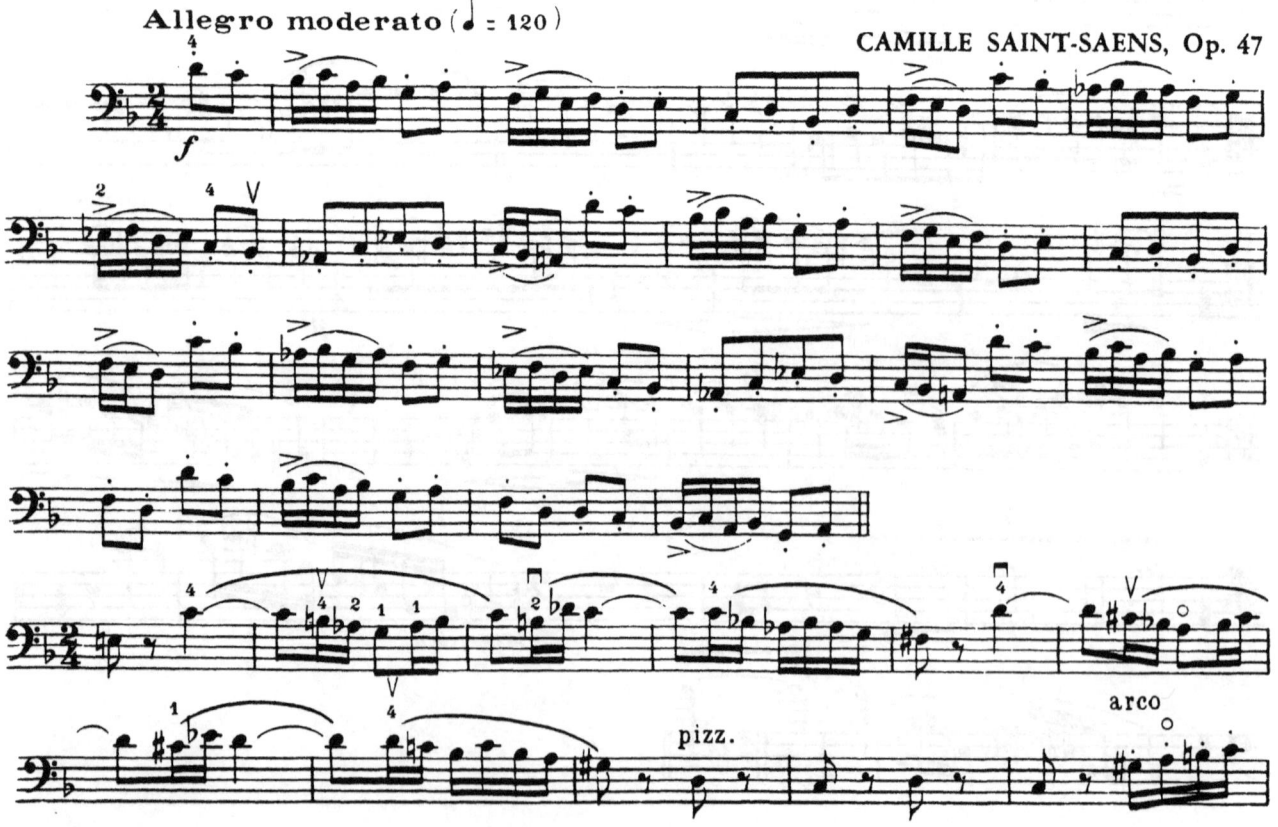

SYMPHONY No. 8
(Unfinished)

FRANZ SCHUBERT

SYMPHONY No. 1

ROBERT SCHUMANN, Op. 38

Allegro molto vivace

Larghetto

Allegro animato e grazioso

Overture "MANFRED"

In leidenschaftlichem Tempo ♩= 144

ROBERT SCHUMANN, Op. 115

SYMPHONY No. 1

DMITRI SHOSTAKOVICH, Op. 10

SYMPHONY No. 1

JEAN SIBELIUS, Op. 39

The Swan of Tuonela

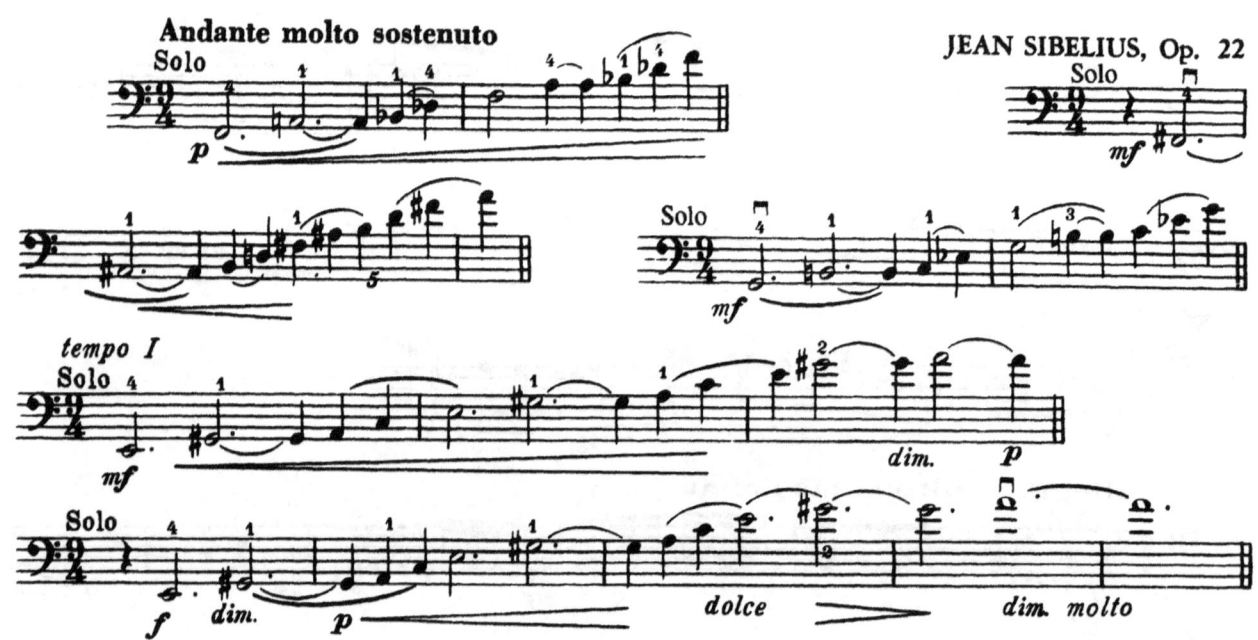

MOLDAU

Emperor Waltz

JOHANN STRAUSS, Op. 437

PETROUCHKA

IGOR STRAVINSKY

Overture "Poet and Peasant"

FRANZ v. SUPPÉ

THE SWAN LAKE

Tempo di Valse PETER TCHAIKOVSKY, Op. 20

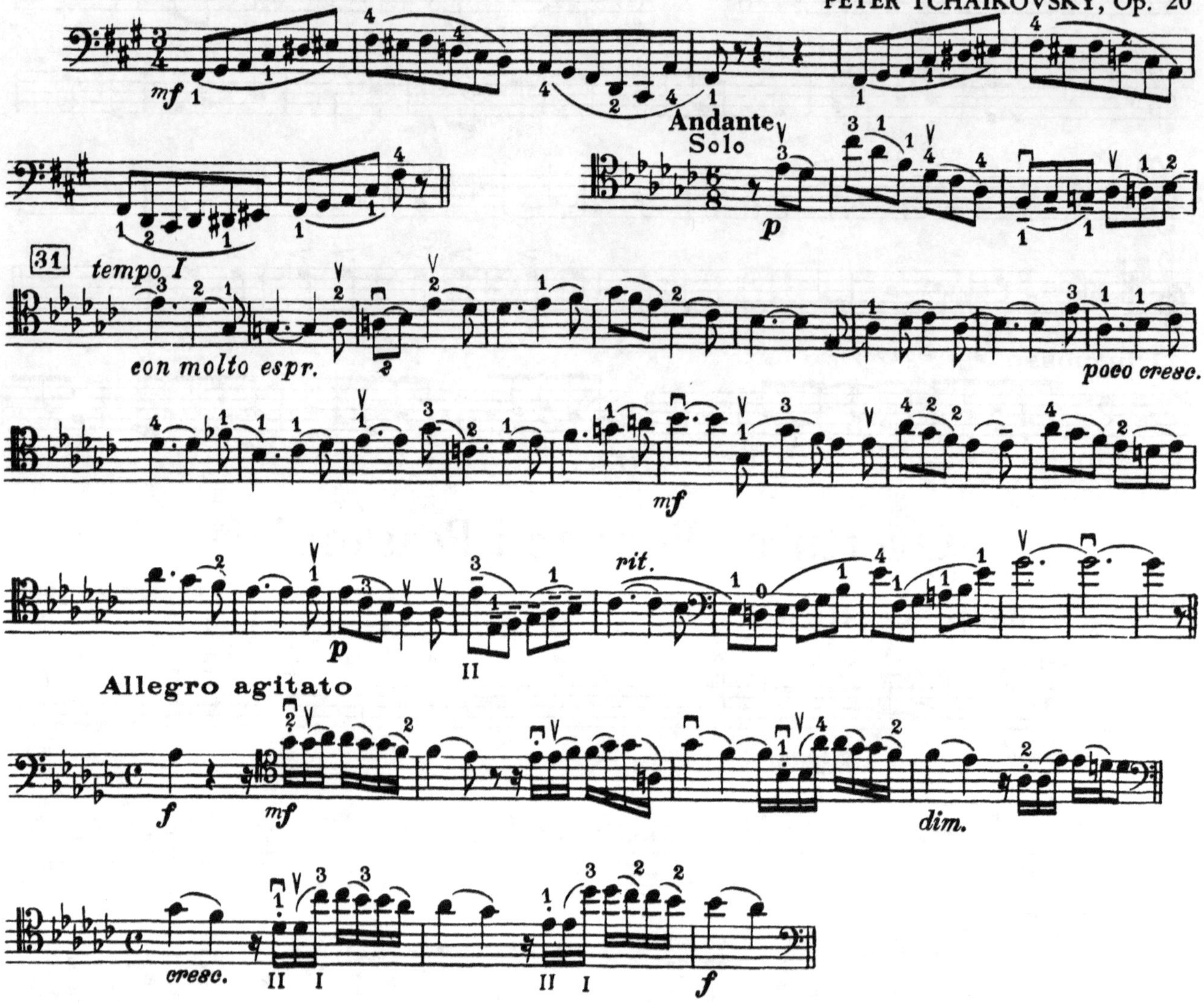

SYMPHONY No. 4

Moderato
con anima (♩. = In movimento di Valse) PETER TCHAIKOVSKY, Op. 36

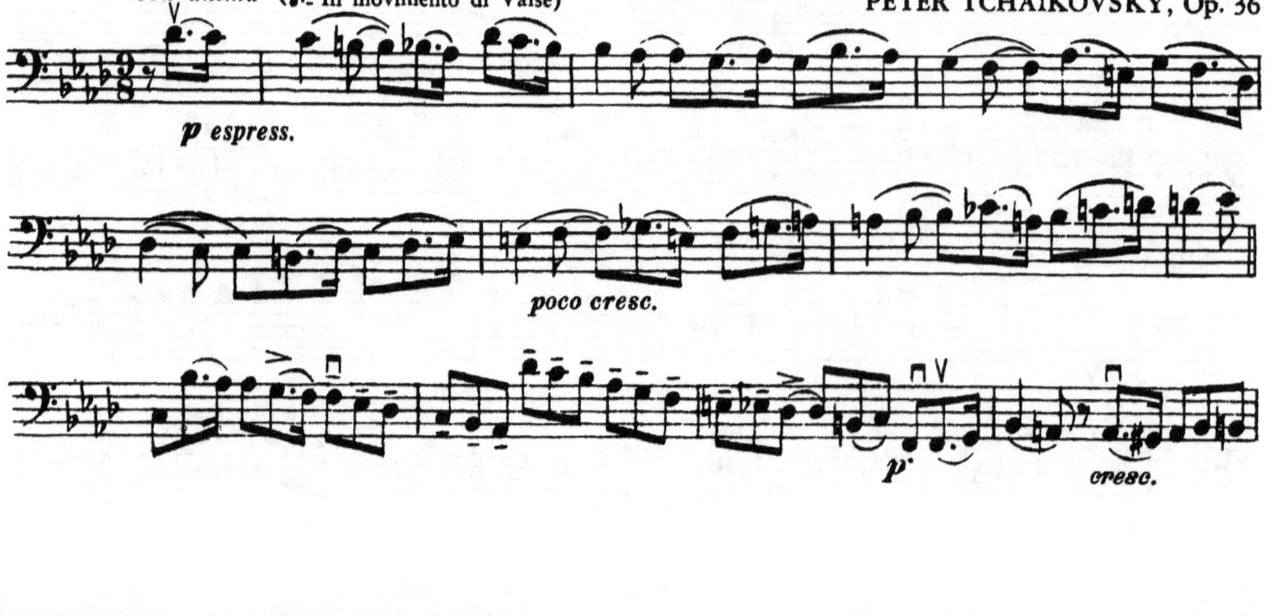

56

Nutcracker Suite

Tempo di Trepak molto vivace

PETER TCHAIKOVSKY, Op. 71a

Tempo di Valse

FAUST OVERTURE

RICHARD WAGNER

Overture "OBERON"

Adagio sostenuto — **Allegro con fuoco**

CARL MARIA v. WEBER

www.ingramcontent.com/pod-product-compliance
Lightning Source LLC
LaVergne TN
LVHW061343060426
835512LV00016B/2652